Little Dog Poems

by Kristine O'Connell George
Illustrated by June Otani

Clarion Books ⚬ New York

Clarion Books
a Houghton Mifflin Company imprint
215 Park Avenue South, New York, NY 10003
Text copyright © 1999 by Kristine O'Connell George
Illustrations copyright © 1999 by June Otani

The text for this book was set in 18/24-point Guardi.
The illustrations for this book were executed in watercolor.

Printed in Singapore.

Library of Congress Cataloging-in-Publication Data

George, Kristine O'Connell.
Little dog poems / by Kristine O'Connell George ; illustrated by June Otani.
p.   cm.
Summary: Short poems present a day in the life of a little dog and its owner.
ISBN 0-395-82266-1
1. Children's poetry, American. 2. Dogs—Juvenile poetry.
[1. Dogs—Poetry. 2. American poetry.]   I. Otani, June, ill.
II. Title.
PS3557.E488L5   1999
811'.54—dc21   97-46678
CIP
AC

TWP   10 9 8 7 6 5 4 3 2 1

For furry and feathered friends Abby, Annie Laurie, Blacky, Blossom, Bo, Buffy, Buster, Caitlin, Cassidy, Celeste, Charlie, Chloe, Cupid, Dinsdale, Dixie, Dora, Dude, Guinevere, Hoss, Jackie, Jessie, Kaycie, King, L.C., Lollipop, Meggie, Mitzi, Mocha, Mugwumps, Nellie, Okie, Orange Julius, Peaches, Peggy, Pepper, Peppy, Pita, Poncho, Pretzel, Puff, Quackie, Roscoe, Rosie, Sadie, Samtoo, Shiloh, Skippy, Spi, Spri, Susie, Suzi, Taran, Terry, Tolstoi, and Zeke.

—K.O.G.

For Lauren Kyoko and furry friends Jasper, Hektor, Aki, Maggie, Rhett, Shadow, Shady, Monty, Jeremiah, Candy, Charlie, Molly, Max, Tabitha, Cosette, Willoughby, Niki, Rudy, Mazie, Bosun, Matilda, Jack, and Putter.

—J.O.

Cold Nose

Little Dog's cold nose
is better than any

alarm clock.

Reflection

Little Dog barks
at the mirror,
trying to get
that other
little dog
to come out
to play.

Enemy

Little Dog barks and chases
the noisy enemy
around the house

until the vacuum
learns its lesson
and stops growling.

Sentinel

Little Dog wants
to see what is
going on outside.

I move a chair
to the front window,
so Little Dog
can supervise
the neighborhood.

Ground Traffic Control

Little Dog had a
busy morning.

One mail jeep.
One delivery truck.
A cat.

Morning Nap

Little Dog curls up tighter and tighter until Little Dog is exactly the same size as the sunny spot.

Mail Delivery

Little Dog proudly carries in the mail,

one

     letter

         at

            a

               time.

Air Traffic Control

Shhhh.

Little Dog must rest
after chasing
that airplane

      away.

Car Ride

Racing
from window
to window,
Little Dog barks
at all those other cars
that are chasing us.

Obedience School

Other dogs heel.
   Little Dog sits.

Other dogs lie down.
   Little Dog sits.

Other dogs sit.
   Little Dog sits.

At last I can say,
   Good dog, Little Dog!

Catch

I taught Little Dog to play
    Catch.

Little Dog is teaching me to play
    Chase.

Warrior

Little Dog barks
to call me
to witness
the triumph—

one cornered beetle.

Wisdom

Little Dog
approaches
new corners
care
     f
     u
     l
     l
     y.

Gardener

I plant tulips.
Little Dog plants a bone.

I pull up weeds.
Little Dog unplants
    one marigold
    and three pansies.

Bath

Dripping and soggy,
Little Dog
really is

little.

The Best Ball

Little Dog has six
yellow tennis balls,
all the very same.

The best ball
is the one

under the bed.

Birthday

Only someone
who loves Little Dog
very much
would bake
birthday cookies with

liver powder.

Hide and Seek

Little Dog hides
dog cookies
behind the couch.

Little Dog looks
behind the couch.
Surprise!
Dog cookies!

Leaving

Little Dog hates keys
    and purses
    and suitcases
    and backpacks—

all the things that mean

goodbye.

Coming Home

Happy to see me?

Is that why you
are jumping so high,
trying to turn
yourself
inside out?

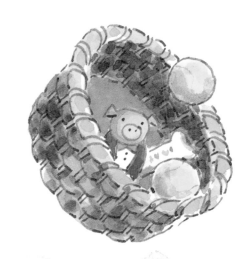

Presents

Little Dog snoops
in the bag
from the pet store.

How did Little Dog know
I brought home
a present?

Mystery

Little Dog is
not allowed
on the beds.

Who made this
warm round dent
in my quilt?

Thief

Oh, Dog.

I bought you toys.

Why my new socks?

Evening

Little Dog sits quietly
by the screen door,
peering into the darkness,

waiting for the breeze
to bring the evening news
from the neighborhood.

Kitchen

Little Dog watches
   chopping
   and stirring

with one big thought:

Drop.

Comfort

A flannel pillow
stuffed with sawdust.
A bone with meat.
A family.

Life is good.

Cozy

Little Dog tugs
an enormous pillow
all the way across the room
to sit beside the fire
with me.

Oops!

Little Dog is not allowed
to have people food.

Sometimes
I have accidents
with my
popcorn.

Scratch

Little Dog nudges and bumps,
Little Dog's tail wags,
and Little Dog's leg twitches,
to let me know I've found

the itchy place.

Bedtime

No one will ever guess
that the lump
under my blanket is

Little Dog.